HARD TIMES

Peter Brookes

WE'RE ALL IN — TIGHTEN YOUR BELTS — THIS TOGETHER

The Robson Press

For Angela, Ben and Will

First published in Great Britain in 2011 by
The Robson Press
Biteback Publishing Ltd
Westminster Tower
3 Albert Embankment
London
SE1 7SP

ISBN 978-1-849541-74-9

10 9 8 7 6 5 4 3 2 1

Printed and bound in Great Britain by Butler Tanner & Dennis Ltd

Foreword
By Matthew Parris

One of the things that makes *Times* readers and writers feel part of the same club is that we all, almost without exception, adore Peter Brookes. The reader may turn straight to the Brookes cartoon without even reading the headlines; we who write the paper do the same. Peter can hardly enter the lift at *The Times* without a colleague rounding on him and demanding in a ho-ho voice: 'And who have you got in your sights for tomorrow, Peter?'

I belong to the 'I know what I like' school of cartoon appreciation. So, asked to speak at the opening of an exhibition of Peter's work at the Chris Beetles gallery in London, I racked my brains for something more expert to say than that I think Brookes is brilliant. How does he hit his mark so unerringly? How does he draw his audience in, in such a good-natured way, while also being (at times) unbelievably vicious? Why do politicians queue to bid for Brookes originals, even when they are the target?

Stumped for an answer, and finding myself in a restaurant in the West End, I spotted Kenneth Baker across the room. He is in the Lords now, but as a senior minister in the last Conservative government he was more often to be found in the cartoons, and depicted in *Spitting Image* (to his delight) as a slug. Lord Baker has become one of Britain's leading collectors and connoisseurs of cartoon and caricature in political satire, publishing some splendid studies of the savagery of the English cartoon under George III and George IV. He knows his cartoon onions.

So I made my way across to his table. 'Tell me something knowledgeable to say about Brookes. I can't just say he is good.'

An email popped up a few days later: 'My view is that Peter Brookes is the most intelligent of our cartoonists; and the mind is just as important as the ability to draw. With other contemporary cartoonists you know exactly where they are coming from but Peter is much more subtle. He can be equally cruel to all parties and equally kind to them. He combines astute political comment with superb caricature. He is undoubtedly the best draughtsman of the lot and is very clever at positioning his drawings in the given space. His cartoons put the message across very precisely without the writing...'

Can I add to that? Yes. It wouldn't quite be right to say that Peter projects no opinion of his own. You cannot have followed his draughtsmanship on the Iraq War, for example, without noticing that he feels intensely. That his view directly and consistently contradicted the editorial line of the newspaper publishing him is a tribute to both. But what you never feel about Peter is that he is rooting for one political team or against another. He is not tribal.

With *The Guardian*'s Steve Bell, for instance (another cartoonist I admire enormously), you do notice that he takes sides. Steve loathes the Tories. Peter is different. His target is rarely the ideology of one politician or another. It is the vanity, inanity and mediocrity of the whole damn lot. He understands, from the poacher's side of the fence, what I came to understand on the gamekeeper's side, that politicians resemble each other in more ways than they differ. They are all, as Peter might himself observe, in the same zoo.

But I omitted Ken Baker's final remark. 'Future generations,' Baker concludes, 'will collect Brookes.'

Death of Senator Edward Kennedy; his presidential ambitions were scuppered by the Chappaquiddick incident.

MP Sir Peter Viggers' duck house becomes emblematic of the MPs' expenses scandal.

The leader of the British National Party, Nick Griffin, makes a highly controversial appearance on BBC1's *Question Time*.

HAITI PRE-QUAKE... HAITI POST-QUAKE... HAITI RECONSTRUCTION...

Catholic convert Tony Blair appears before the Chilcot Inquiry into the war in Iraq.

The Chilcot Inquiry.

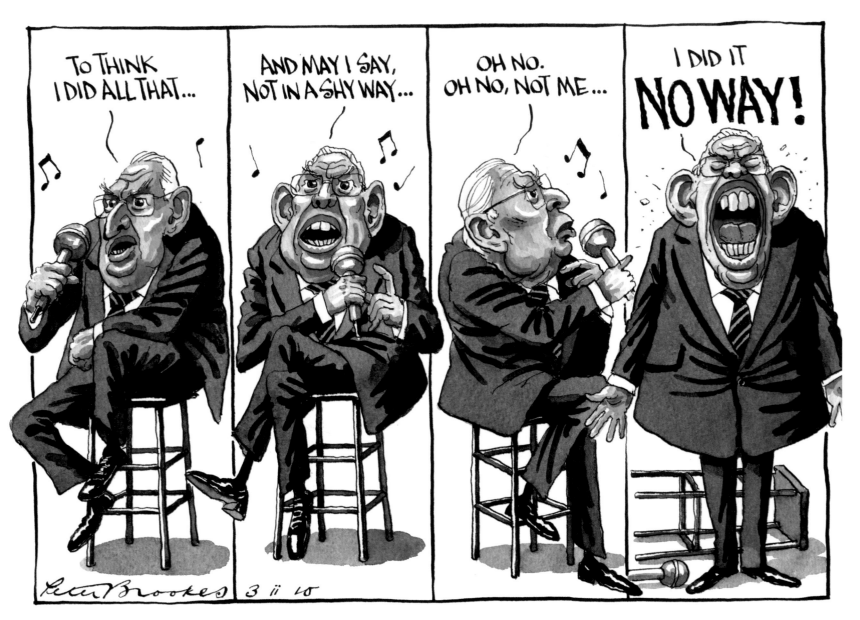

The Rev. Ian Paisley, former leader of the Democratic Unionist Party of Northern Ireland, announces he will step down as an MP.

The nuclear ambitions of Mahmoud Ahmadinejad's Iran cause Obama and Putin concern.

The first Greek bailout.

Lord Ashcroft is a significant contributor to the Conservatives' 2010 election coffers.

MPs investigate Conservative Party donor Lord Ashcroft's tax status, as US artist
Spencer Tunick unveils his latest installations involving large groups of nudes.

Obama passes his Healthcare Bill at the last gasp.

Tony Blair makes his only appearance in the 2010 election campaign.

Gordon Brown talks up the economy during the 2010 election campaign.

Gordon Brown's open mic gaffe on the election trail.

The last day of Gordon Brown's 2010 election campaign.

The first day of the coalition.

NATURE NOTES

Yellow-billed Oxpecker
(*Libdemos soldoutus*)

These small birds live off large mammals in a symbiotic relationship, known as mutualism. They cleanse their host while feeding on ticks and fleas. But far from working for the common good, they are in reality scavenging bottom-feeders.

15 4 20

Peter Brookes

The state opening of Parliament: the Queen announces cuts to the Royal Family's expenditure.

Education Secretary Michael Gove sets out a policy of allowing 'free' schools.

Following the Gulf of Mexico oil spill, President Obama meets BP chief executives in the Oval Office.

Nick Clegg struggles to defend the progessive credentials of the Emergency Budget.

The Queen and the Duke of Edinburgh, visiting America, face up to life after Civil List payments are frozen.

25

Education Secretary Michael Gove in trouble as plans to cancel a school
building programme are leaked, in contrast to his Labour shadow.

John Prescott is elevated to the House of Lords.

Grim news on the death toll from Afghanistan and the oil leak in the Gulf of Mexico.

Tony Blair was allegedly annoyed – on several counts – by Peter Mandelson's decision to publish his memoirs.

The Lib Dems continue to suffer the lion's share of criticism of coalition policies.

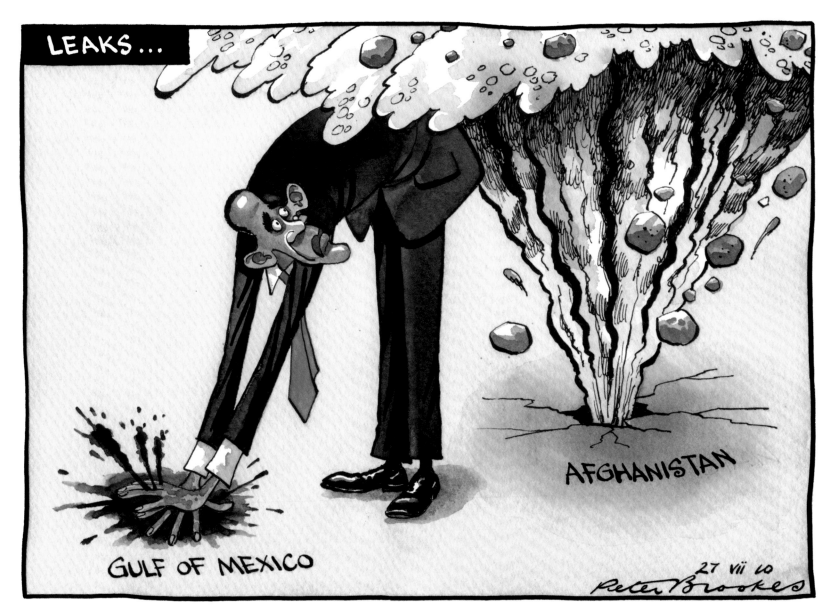

LEAKS...

GULF OF MEXICO

AFGHANISTAN

27 vii 10

Peter Brookes

Wikileaks exposes Afghan military secrets as the oil spill in the Gulf of Mexico continues.

Pope Benedict XVI visits the UK.

The Lib Dem conference in Liverpool.

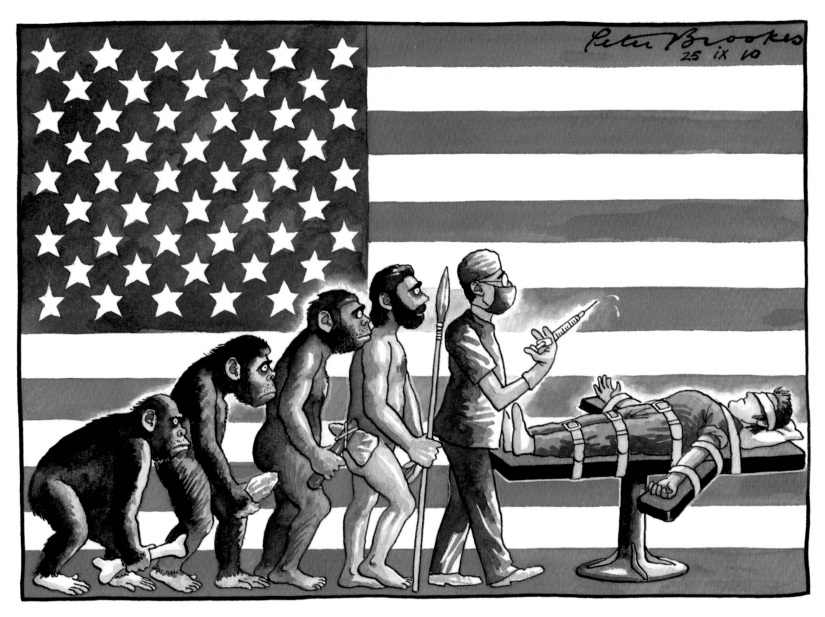

American Teresa Lewis executed by lethal injection.

Ed Miliband beats his brother in the election to become Labour leader.

David Miliband refuses to serve his younger brother in the shadow cabinet.

Chancellor George Osborne promises to 'put fuel in the tank of the British economy'.

Vince Cable announces the part privatisation of the Royal Mail, as the saga of the trapped Chilean miners draws to a close.

George Osborne announces cuts to disability benefits.

Business Secretary Vince Cable spells out his programme.

Halloween: London Mayor Boris Johnson attacks David Cameron over housing policy.

Cameron and Sarkozy sign defence and nuclear joint-working treaties.

Obama's Democrats lose control of Congress as a Tea Party-inspired right sweep the US mid-term elections.

Human rights are not top of David Cameron's agenda as he visits China.

Today presenter James Naughtie 'misspeaks' as he introduces Culture Secretary Jeremy Hunt.

Student riots in London coincide with the awarding of the Nobel Peace Prize.

As allegations fly following the Giffords shooting in Arizona, Sarah Palin, whose campaigns had featured a gunsight crosshairs motif, rejects any share of the blame for inflaming the political debate.

Conservative rebel David Davis criticises Cameron over social mobility.

The first day of the Egyptian demonstrations.

The Arab Spring. But despite the protests, President Mubarak of Egypt refuses to relinquish power...

... until he does.

Italian Premier Berlusconi is under fire for his infamous 'Bunga Bunga' parties.

DAFTA

BEST DIRECTOR IN A COMPLETELY INCOHERENT FOREIGN LANGUAGE... 'THE BIG SOCIETY'

As the Arab Spring dawns, Britain has a large presence at a major arms fair.

Cameron and Clegg give opposing speeches on the Alternative Vote referendum.

The beginning of action in Libya.

As Nick Clegg's Lib Dems are bruised in the Darlington by-election, the country debates the imposition of a no-fly zone over Libya.

A furore erupted over Prince Andrew's role as a UK trade ambassador, as the past of some of his acquaintances emerged.

The aftermath of the Japanese tsunami.

66

As cuts bite across the board on the domestic front, Britain launches another military campaign, against Gaddafi's Libya.

Inflation disrupts George Osborne's Budget plans.

Nick Clegg's speech on social mobility fails to dampen accusations of hypocrisy over the Lib Dems' U-turn on tuition fees.

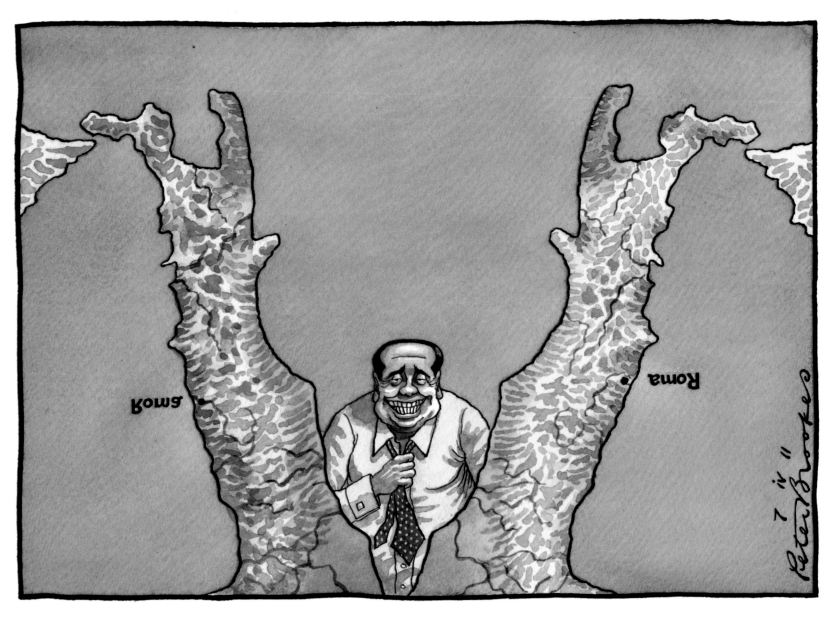

The opening of the trial of Italian Premier Silvio Berlusconi on charges that he paid for sex with an under-age prostitute.

A ban on face coverings comes into force in France.

Colonel Gaddafi proves more difficult to overthrow than anticipated.

Hague delivers a speech promising that British intervention in Libya would continue until Gaddafi goes.

NO BOOTS ON THE GROUND...

21 iv 11 Peter Brookes

Foreign Secretary William Hague's terms of engagement for Libya.

The Royal Wedding coincides with focus on the practice of celebrities obtaining 'super injunctions' to gag the press.

Osama bin Laden, mastermind of the 9/11 attacks, is killed in a US raid on his compound in Pakistan.

Conspiracy theories abound after the news of Osama bin Laden's death.

As President Obama attends a wreath laying ceremony at Ground Zero, he
reaps the political capital attendant on the assassination of Osama bin Laden.

Nick Clegg expounds new Liberal thinking.

Doubt is expressed over the veracity of material recovered from Osama bin Laden's HQ.
(Historian Hugh Trevor-Roper infamously authenticated the faked Hitler diaries.)

There is speculation that DSK's arrest springs from anti-French sentiment on the part of the Americans.

The Queen and Duke of Edinburgh's State Visit to Ireland.

As International Monetary Fund Chief (and possible contender for the French Presidency) Dominique
Strauss-Kahn is arrested in New York on sexual assault charges, Nicolas Sarkozy sees the political upside.

Nick Clegg is denied a one-on-one meeting with Barack Obama.

Cameron entertains US President Barack Obama at 10 Downing Street.

Bosnian Serb leader Ratko Mladic finally arrested for war crimes.

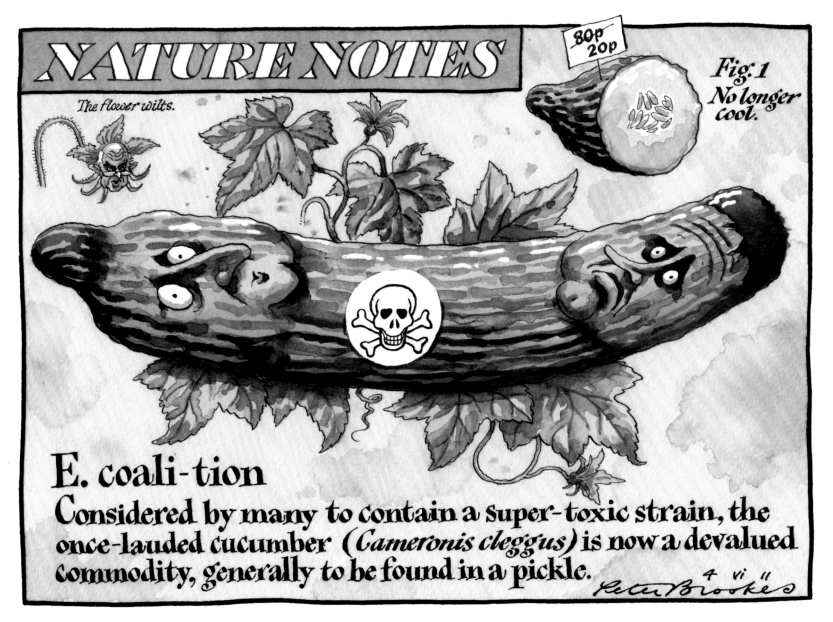

Strains between No. 10 and the Deputy Prime Minister's Office coincide with an outbreak of *E. coli* in Germany.

E. coli and Eurozone crises continue.

The Archbishop of Canterbury criticises the 'Big Society'.

The Duke of Edinburgh celebrates his 90th birthday.

Clegg celebrates victory over NHS reforms.

The difficulty of getting rid of Gaddafi, as Northern Irish golfer Rory McIlroy wins the US Open.

German Chancellor Angela Merkel is central to a second bailout of the Greek economy.

Questions over Miliband's leadership after he calls for the abolition of shadow cabinet elections.

Cameron is happy to do business with China while berating Arab leaders for human rights abuses.

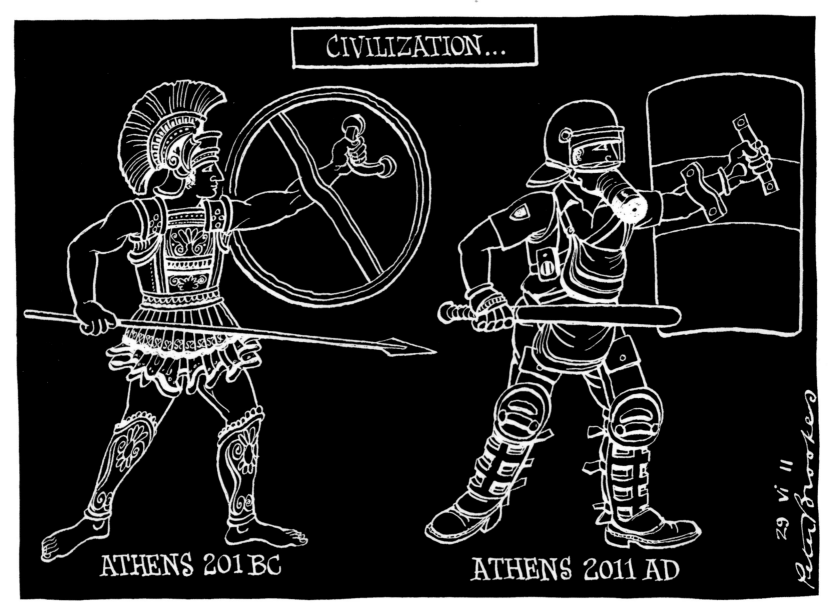

Riots in Athens as the Greek economy collapses.

The Horn of Africa suffers devastating famine.

The *News of the World* folds.

Brown, Cameron and Miliband were once happy to take Murdoch's hospitality.

101

News International Chief Executive Rebekah Brooks resigns.

As the phone hacking scandal starts to claim senior police scalps, Rupert Murdoch is attacked with a foam pie while giving evidence to a House of Commons Select Committee.

In Norway, Anders Behring Breivik massacres sixty-nine at a youth camp.

As the one-year countdown to the Olympics commences, growth figures of 0.2 per cent are released.